THE ALL NEW STYLE OF MAGAZINE-BOOKS

SDM

www.SDMLIVE.com

MP

MOCY PUBLISHING
WWW.MOCYPUBLISHING.COM

SDM

EDITOR-IN-CHIEF
D. "Casino" Bailey
casino@sdmlive.com

EDITORAL DIRECTOR
Sheree Cranford
sheree@sdmlive.com

GRAPHIC/WEB DESIGNER
D. "Casino" Bailey
casino@sdmlive.com

A&R MANAGER
Aye Money
ayemoney@sdmlive.com

ACCOUNT EXECUTIVE
Frank Harvest Jr.
frank@sdmlive.com

PHOTOGRAPHERS
Treagen Colston
D. "Casino" Bailey

CONTRIBUTORS
April Smiley
Courtney Benjamin

COPY ORDERS & ADVERTISING OFFICE
Send Money Order or Check to:
Mocy Publishing
P.O. Box 35195
Detroit, Michigan 48235
(586) 646-8505
advertise@sdmlive.com

Copy Order Item #:
SDM Magazine Issue #2 2015
S&H Plus Retail Price - $9.99 per copy

WWW.SDMLIVE.COM

Printed by CreateSpace, An Amazon.com Company

MP
MOCY PUBLISHING

REAL MUSIC. REAL ENTERTAINMENT.

SDM

ISSUE 2.

ALSO
BIG SEAN
JADE JUDO
ARMORNITION
JP ONE
ESKO

DJBJ
MIXTAPE AND RADIO SUPERSTAR DROPS A FEW WORDS FOR NEW MUSIC ARTIST

LYNN CARTER
BRINGS THE R&B BACK TO THE GAME WITH HER INSPIRATIONAL SOUND AND SEXY NEW LOOK

PLUS MORE

ROBERT CURRY
RELEASING ALL NEW MUSIC AND MAKING IT WITHOUT THE BAND

SPOTIFY PAYS OUT
HOW PERRIN LAMB EARNED OVER $56K FROM ONE SONG ON SPOTIFY

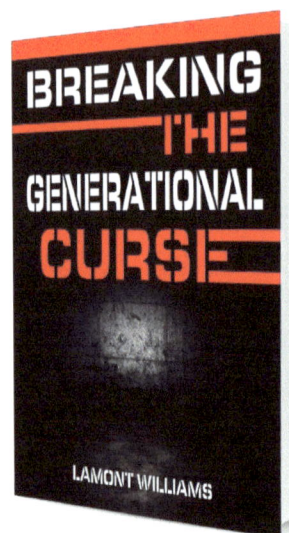

CONTENTS

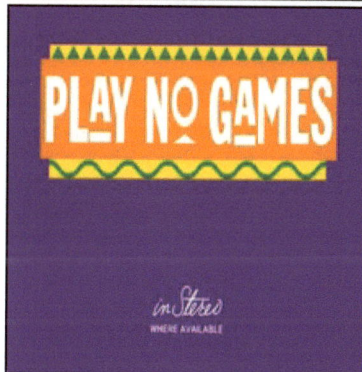

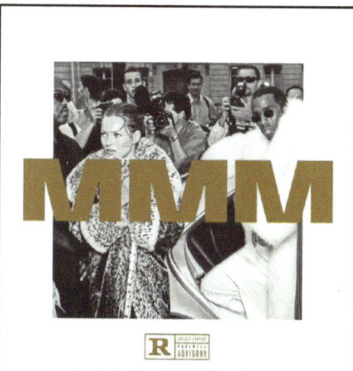

1

UHD TV
Ultra High Definition 4K

NEW ELECTRONICS

A LIST OF SOME OF THE PICK'S THIS MONTH.

BY JEFF WALKER

2

1 Samsung - 55" Smart 4K Ultra HD TV

Check out the Samsung 4K Ultra HD TV, the world's newest addition to PurColor Technology. The Samsung 4K Ultra HD TV also allows you to watch TV using the built-in Wi-Fi. You can stream music and download apps on the TV.

2 Apple TV

Get access to instant entertainment with the Apple TV. Just connect to the Internet and stream movies, listen to music, and access a wide variety of other content. You can also connect your iPhone or iPad to the Apple TV for streaming more apps.

3

3 WowWee - MiP Robot

The WowWee MiP 0825 robot is a robot that plays games, drives, dances, battles, balances, responds to motions. This is all controlled remotely controlled by a compatible iOS or Android cell phone for ease of use. The dual wheels allow smooth, simple mobility.

4 LG - ChromeBase 21.5" All-In-One - Intel Celeron

This LG ChromeBase 22CV241-W all-in-one computer features built-in wireless networking and a 1.3MP webcam, which makes it simple to chat with family and friends over the Internet. The Intel® Celeron® processor is reliable for everyday computing.

4

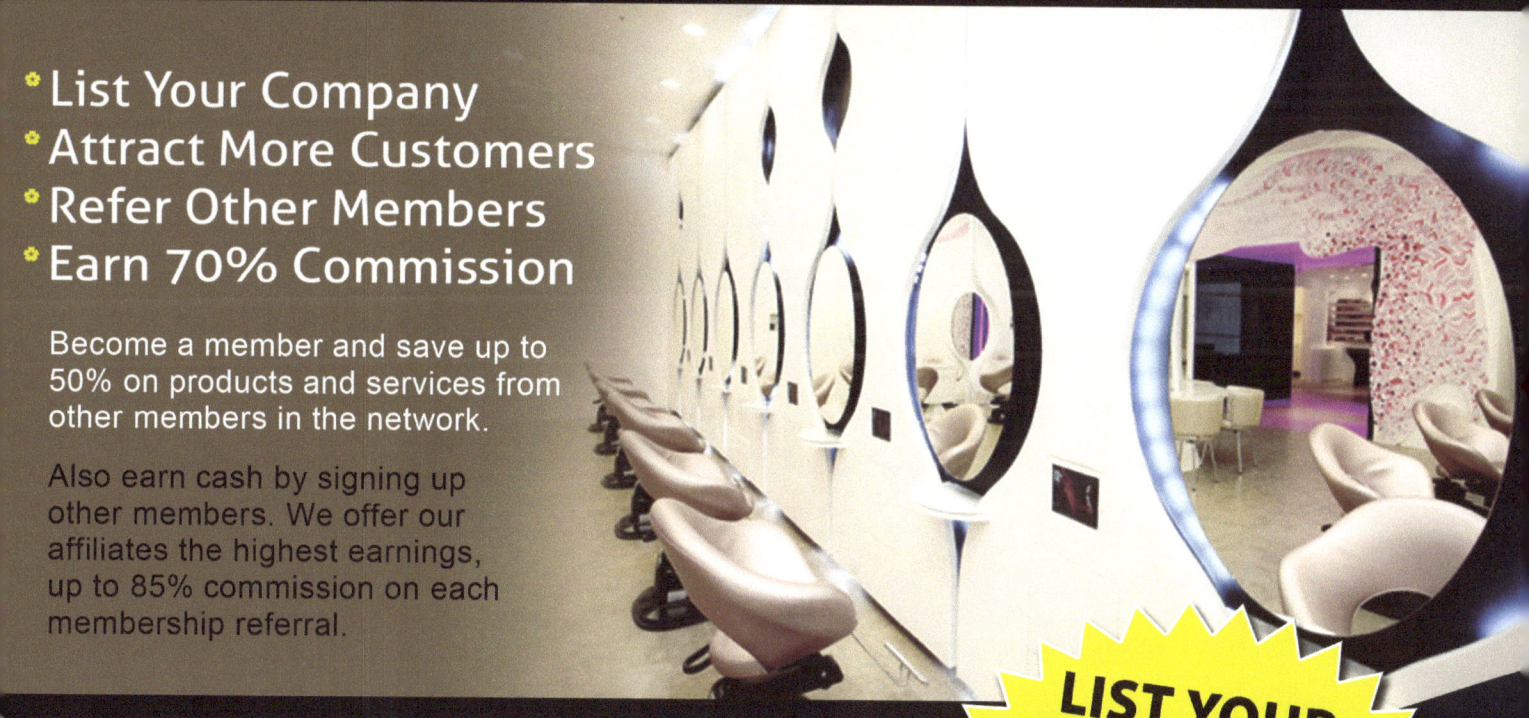

The biggest thing to happen to iPhone since iPhone.

iPhone 6s

www.apple.com

Big Sean Reps The 313

REPPING DETROIT IS RAPPER BIG SEAN AND HE'S DOING BIG THINGS THESE DAYS. OPENING FOR THE LIONS HALF-TIME IS JUST A TASTE.

by Colin Stutz

Big Sean doesn't once again by shutting down a half-time show at the Detroit Lions game 11/27/2015 against the Philadelphia Eagles. Sean walks in the stadium with the crowd of kids rapping is hit single "One Man Can Change The World" and grace the stage with another hit "Blessing". Unfortunately, Drake and Kanye West wasn't there to help with the performance, the show was still B.I.G.

This man is unbreakable and this highlights a huge step in Big Sean's career as of the date.

Big Sean

Loud Gang

Sweeping through the D with their hardcore rap flow is the eastside group Loud Gang. The group includes Rich Boy, Den, Dela, and Rock. A few of their street bangers include "My Dogs", "Balling," and "All Dem Nights."

You can listen to more tracks from the group on YouTube under GCBLoudgang. Please follow this upcoming group on Instagram and Twitter @Loudgang because they are bound to be the next successful rap group.

The Shadiest Book To Read

CHERAEE C. GIVE'S HER READERS A DOUBLE TAKE AFTER READING HER NEW BOOK TITLED "THE SHADIEST MISSION EVER".

by Carl Winter

Mocy Publishing's top author Cheraee C. is back with another street, spine-chilling tale/her fourth novel "The Shadiest Mission Ever" is the third sequel to her Shady Series (Another Shady Mission, On Another Shady Mission, and now The Shadiest Mission Ever.)

All of her characters are set in their shady ways, living their shady little lifestyles. Her plot is full of unpredictable, gritty events that will leave her readers in awe and corrupted moments of passion. Cheraee C. makes it hard for any of her characters to survive the shady missions in Part 3. This book defies the definition of shady and is the shadiest book you'll ever read.

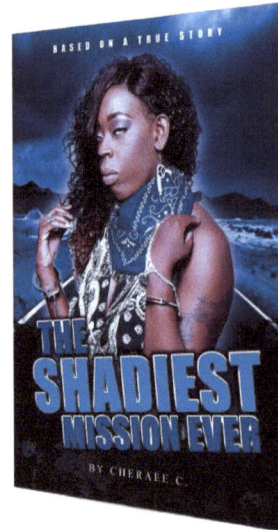

The Shadiest Mission Ever
By Cheraee C.

Available from Amazon.com and other online stores

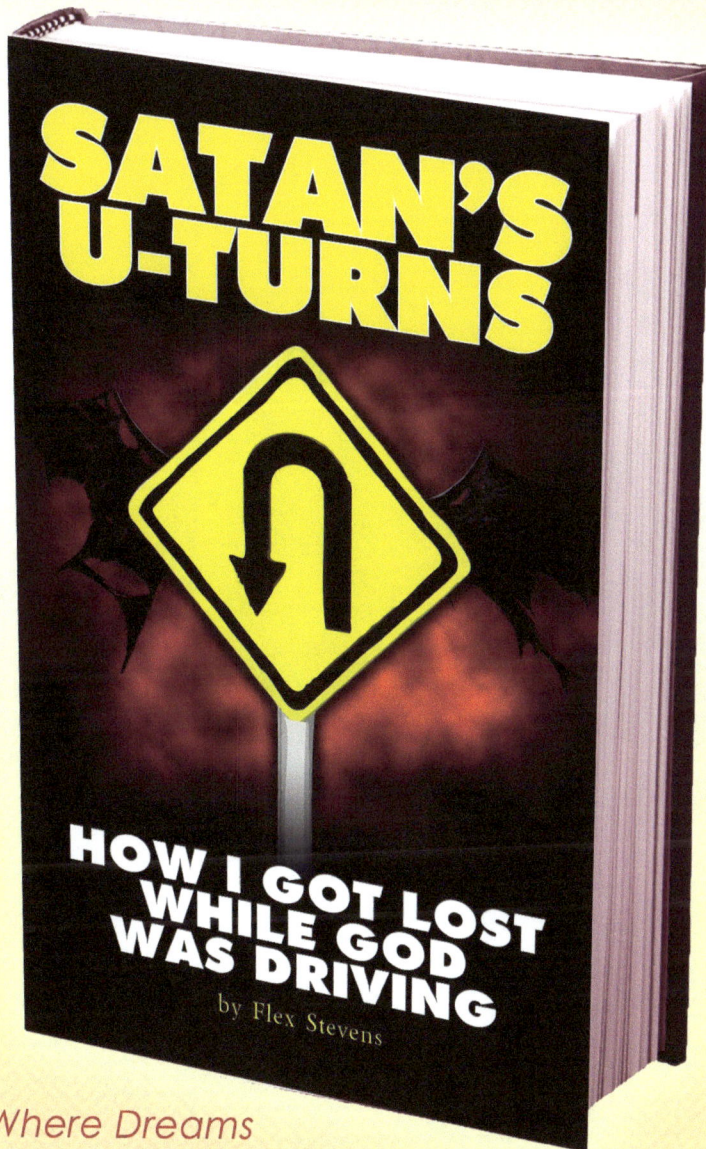

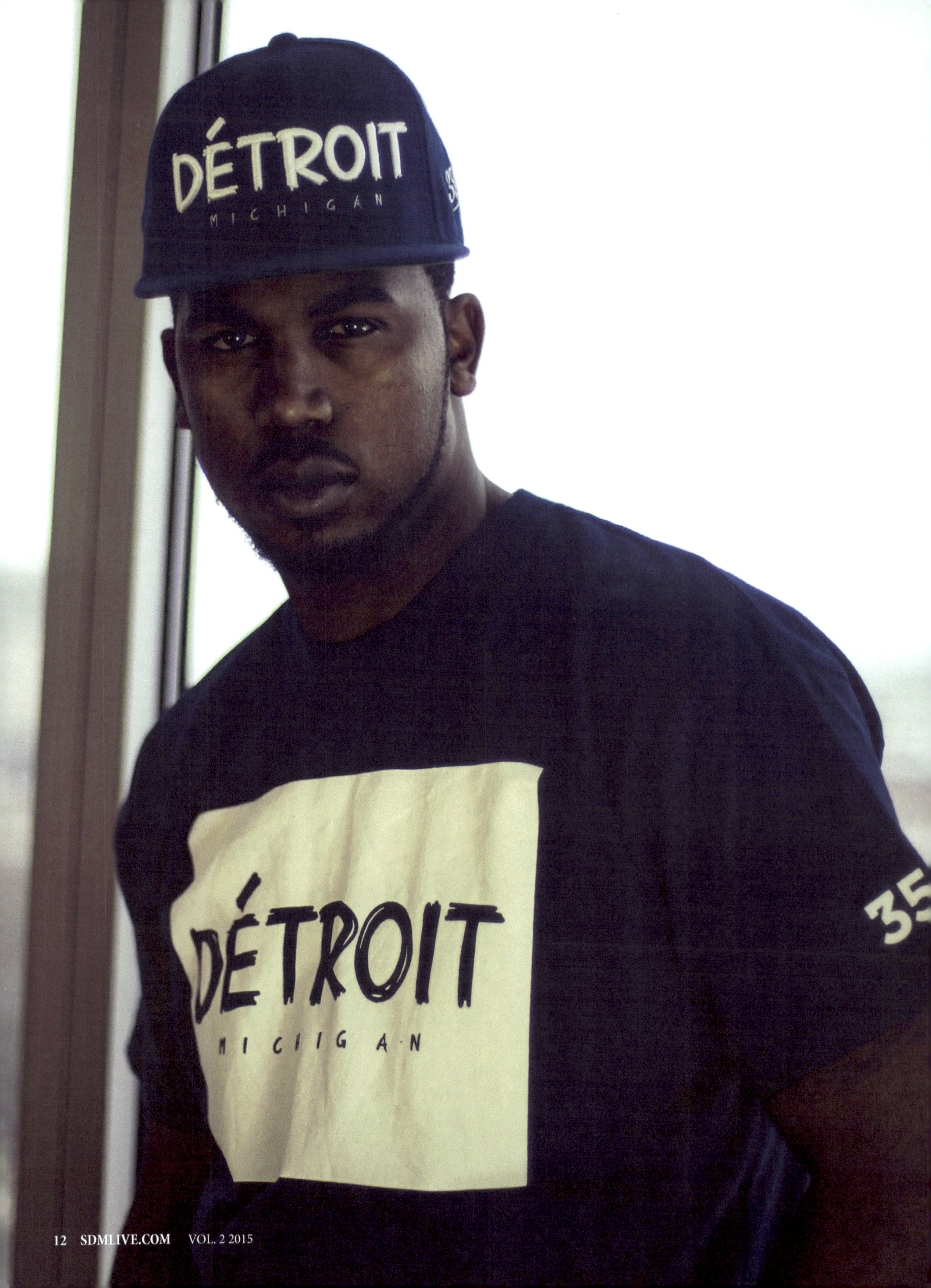
DÉTROIT
MICHIGAN
DÉTROIT
MICHIGAN

Mr. 3525 DjBj Pays Attention

MANAGING AN EMPIRE CAN BE A RUFF TASK BUT DJBJ IS HOLDING IT DOWN WITH A LOT OF OTHER PROJECTS AS WELL.

by Cheraee C.

The illest DJ in the city is hitting every productive market there is, and his name is DJBJ also known as Mr. Pay Attention. You can catch DJBJ live on Hot 107.5 Monday-Friday jamming from 7-12noon. Always on the scope for new talent, DJBJ is at the Bullfrog every other Sunday ready to watch new artists showcase themselves. Step to the Mic and show the city what you got.

DJBJ also plays a profound role in Michigan fashion. His popular, trendy clothing line 3525 is now available in Mr. Alan stores all over Michigan as he just released the Detroit Michigan Collection II. The audience for his line features blue collar workers who are industrious individuals and dress with a hustler's ambition. All of his clothing include Detroit logos and themes. You can check out more exclusive pieces of his line on www.3525clothing.com.

More than just a DJ, host, and a businessman, DJBJ is an artist at heart. During the first quarter of 2016, DJBJ plans to release his latest project "Pardon My Greatness," His single from the album is the westside anthem "Westside" featuring Payroll, Sino, Mez, and Mack Nickels. DJBJ is also making way for the release of Pay Attention Vol. 16 which includes a blend of new Detroit artists mixed with national artists. In 2016, DJBJ will be collaborating on mixtapes with both Icewear Vezzo and Sino.

To all new artists looking for radio play, get your social media game up. Once your fanbase is as big as your dreams, then proposition DJBJ. To observe the cores of DJBJ's diligent life, tune into episodes of his reality series "Life of a DJ" on YouTube. Stay connected with DJBJ on Facebook, Instagram, and Twitter @djbj3525

DjBj & Big Sean

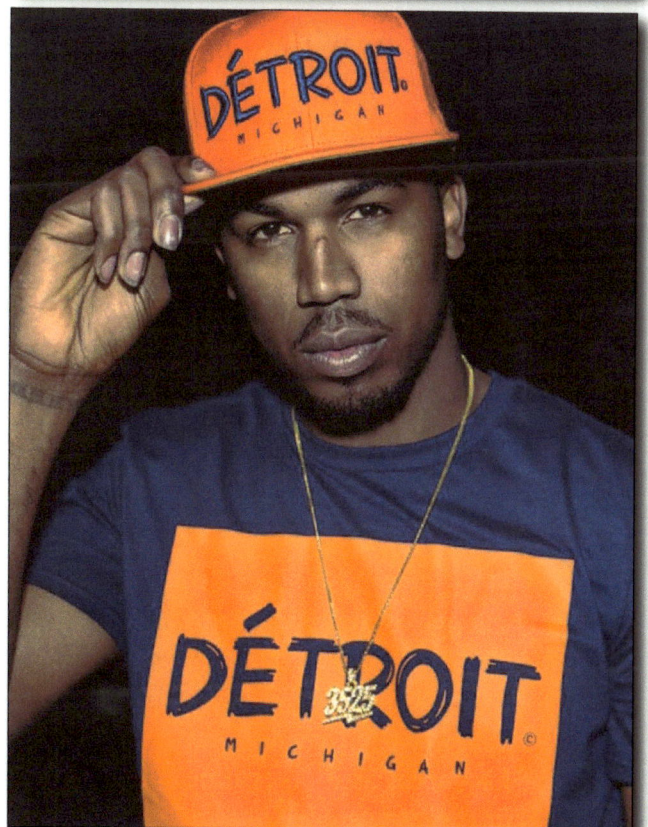

JP One "The Chosen One"

SPEAKS ABOUT HIS HISTORY IN THE MUSIC INDUSTRY AND HOW HE'S CHANGING THE GAME FROM STANDARD TO COMPLEX.

by Cheraee C.

Setting a new standard for aspiring rappers worldwide with bars galore is the Detroit phenomenon JP One. JP One is a strategizer and is an artist with an irrefutable campaign. Not only is he a rapper, but he is an actor and the founder and CEO of his own business Gifted and Talented LLC. He believes that music should have a standard and only exemplifies his music, his atmosphere, and musical affiliates with realism.

JP's first project is titled "The Power of One" released in 2011. His second project is titled "A Beautiful Mind" released in 2012. Following that was his third project titled "Freedom of Speech" also released in 2012 including the Worldstar hit "We Winning." His fourth project is titled "I Am Legend" hosted by DJ Pest released in 2013. His fifth project is titled "Gifted and Talented" which was released in 2014 and received a nomination at Detroit's Hip Hop Awards. JP's most recent project is the Fire and Brimstone Trilogy which includes a three-part series to this concept and all the parts were released in 2015.

A lot of MC's have basic videos that highlight their music. As a result, JP has catchy videos that incorporate acting, skits, and realistic storylines like a mainstream video on BET, VH1, or MTV. With 25 plus notable videos under his belt, you can check out the video for his latest hit single "Runaway" featuring 3D and also "What Will I Do." Everyone can relate to feeling like or actually being a runaway at a semester in their life or just plain being at a standstill.

JP's main challenge as an artist is to continuously increase his fanbase. Second to that is steering rap away from that anything goes type of music because rap is way deeper then modern, frivolous rap. Third, is being the pilot of his career as it takes time and knowledge to progress in the rap game. Consequently, JP is very headstrong and independently making power moves in his musical movement.

Check JP out on Facebook, Instagram, Twitter, Reverb-Nation, and Soundcloud @Chosen1Jackpot. For more information and new music, you can visit JP's website www.jponelife.com. Otherwise, you can catch JP on his third tour coming to a city and a stage near you starting December 2015.

R&B and Hip-Hop Soulful

FROM THE MIDWEST LYNN CARTER IS AN R&B AND HIP-HOP SINGER WITH A LOT OF SOUL AND A SEXY NEW LOOK.

Photography by Cheraee C.

Lynn has been making major-league moves in her career. Lynn has done many song features, and upcoming projects with local MC's, and singers including Young Herk, Shonda Jay, Ray Gifted Keys, Jeiwes, Chris lanard, just to name a few. Lynn is always on the go doing something, whether it's singing, acting, dancing, or modeling, she does it all! Lynn is featuring in the hit stage play "The Lies They Told" By Je'McLin, starring Carl Payne from the hit TV show "Martin", and Tamika Scott from the Grammy award-winning group Xscape, and Zanye, who is a Neo-soul/R&B sensation from Detroit. Lynn has auditioned for walk fashion show and featured in the 2015 Detroit African American festival modeled. Lynn has interviewed with Jason Dixon owner of Detroit's Urban Nation Radio. So, this time next year, she will be singing instead of modeling. Currently, Lynn and Young Herk will be dropping a Christmas song with a twist, with the video to follow. In between time, Lynn performs live with L.a.n.d.i. Ent singing for weddings, Birthday parties, family reunions, funerals and more.

Underway, Lynn has many ventures partaking in 2016. She will be assisting Detroit's own Tiffany Patton on her TV show "On the Go" that airs on the Impact TV Network Comcast Channel 397 and 400. Lynn Carter will be performing again in the stage play "The Lies They Told" which is in Atlanta in 2016. The DVD for the "Lies they Told" will also be coming soon. She will also be performing at the grand opening of Motor City Grill, which is a restaurant coming to Atlanta. Last but not least, Lynn is going to be singing backup vocals for the jazz singer Yancy, who plays for Barack and Michelle Obama.

In 2016, Lynn will be dropping her first mixtape titled "No Dogz Allowed." Her current single is titled "Too Little" featuring Shonda Jay and Kela'MiL, video dropping in 2016. In addition to that, she is working on being a featured artist on an upcoming Support Detroit Movement compilation album.

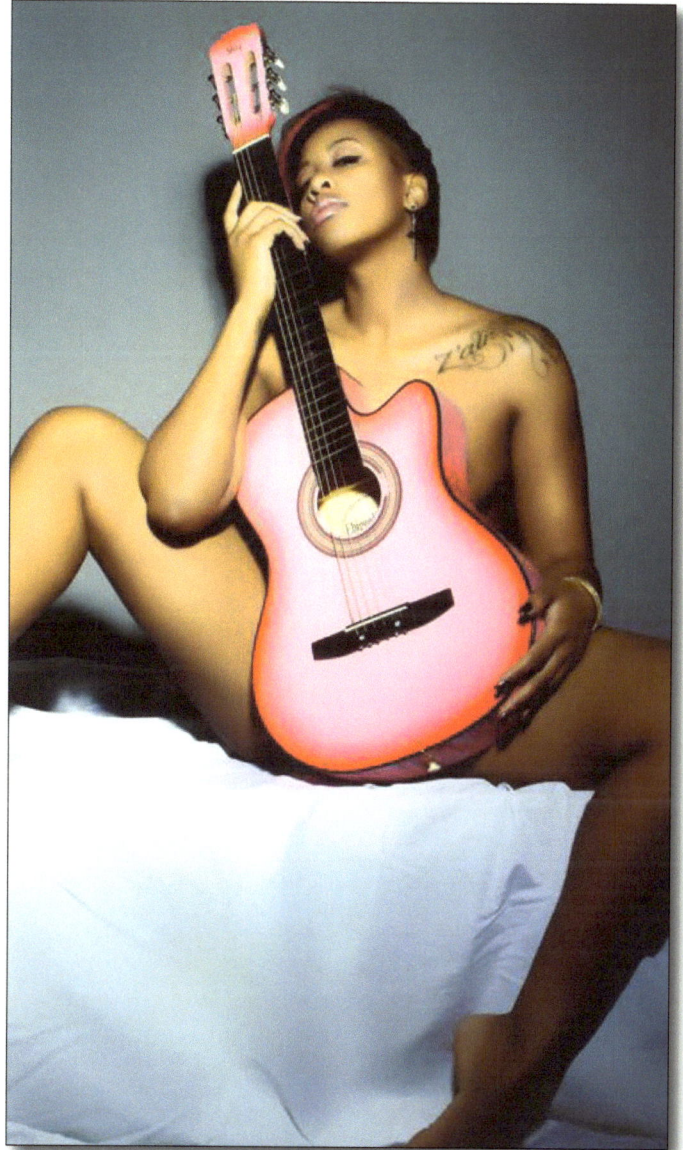

Currently, her music is available on Soundcloud and YouTube and soon to come on a higher platform of music. You can follow this R&B and HipHop sensation on Facebook @Lynn Carter and Instagram @_lynncarter and Twitter @ivycarter041189

Dear God, heal
those with cancer.
Amen.

Spotify News

INDIE ARTIST PERRIN LAMB EARNS OVER $56,000 FROM ONE SONG ON SPOTIFY WITHOUT A RECORD DEAL.

by Semaja Turner

Perrin Lamb is an indie singer-songwriter from Nashville. He's been in music for over a decade. Never signed to a record or publishing deal. He decided to distribute his music thru CD Baby, which an indie music distributor that distributes for independent artists.

In January of 2014, a song that Perrin wrote called "Everyone's Got Something" was selected to feature on the Your Favorite Coffeehouse playlist on Spotify by their editorial team. At this time, Perrin's song had been out for about a year and wasn't doing that well in the industry. It wasn't until the song hit the playlist and boom. The song went from hundreds to millions of plays in no time.

As of today, the song has gained about 13 million streams worldwide. Perrin's was paid for getting over 10,929,203 streams from Spotify for his song "Everyone's Got Something". From that, he earned a total of $40,131.55 (which was left after CD Baby's 9% distribution fee.) Perrin also earned Mechanicals and digital performance royalties that make up the remainder of the total $56,000.

Solo Superstar Robert Curry

HAS DROPPED THE BAND AND IS NOW GIVING THE WORLD SOME NEW R&B/POP MUSIC THAT WE ALL CAN APPRECIATE.

by Cheraee C.

Shining in his very own solo limelight is the singing prodigy from MTV's Making the Band 4, Robert Curry. The Detroit native is on a hot pursuit to rule his industry. Recently, he just migrated from the D to Atlanta, Georgia and floats to L.A. from time to time. Rob is on a mission to reside in the best city where his talents can be magnified and he can be most prosperous as a musician.

There are so many challenges in becoming a solo artist and having a reputation with a popular group. Even though Day 26 is still an entity, Day 26 is just a counterpart of what Rob has to offer. Overflowing with talent and dedication to Day 26, Rob is just chasing his destiny. The journey of acceptance as a solo artist might take some time, but if other artists can pursue solo careers and succeed so can Rob.

Gearing up for his first solo album, Rob released his first single titled "Rehab" which is available on all digital outlets. The song "Rehab" is a very inspirational song Rob wrote himself in which anyone can relate to life and addiction. At the top of the year, Rob will be releasing the music video for the song "Rehab." You can also check out another hot single by Rob titled "Freaky We Are."

Day 26
106 & Park

In 2016, Rob will be returning to reality TV. This time around, Rob will be starring in another show on MTV documenting his come up. Rob is in the business of integrating himself in entirety from his look to his experiences in the music industry. It's time for the world to observe Rob solely as a songwriter, as a producer, as a musician, as a choreographer, and an actor. You can check out the pilot for his upcoming reality show on bossip.com.

You can also follow the face of Michigan's own Voo Vodka, Robert Curry on Instagram@rob_a_curry, on Twitter @ Rob_day26, and on Facebook @Robert A Curry.

ROBERT CURRY
REHAB
FROM FORTHCOMING ALBUM

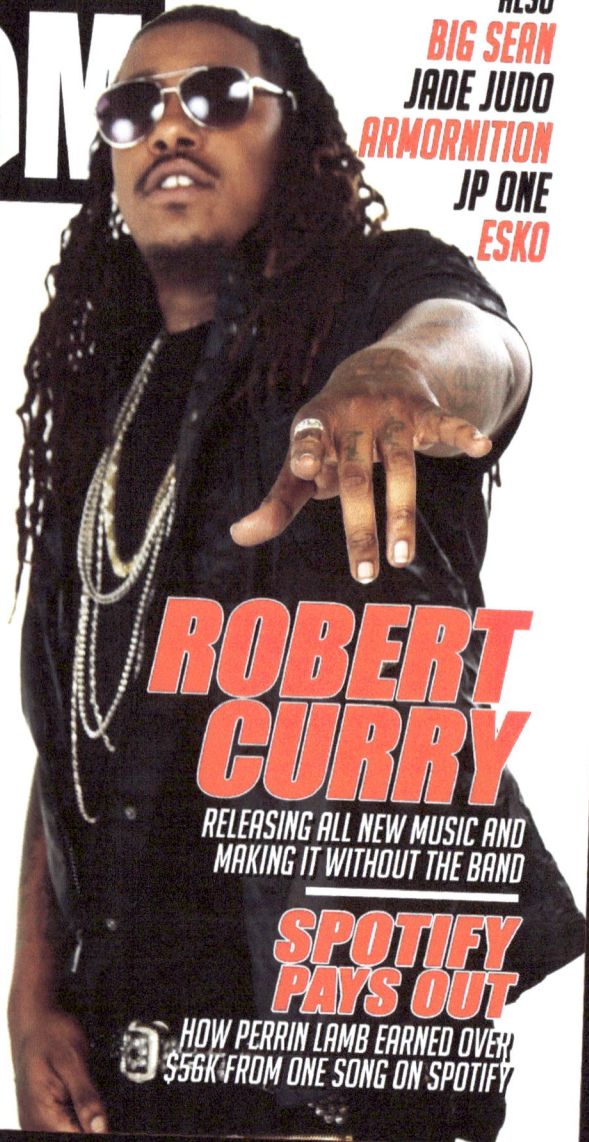

TOP 10 CHARTS

TOP 10 DIGITAL SINGLES AND ALBUMS
DECEMBER 1, 2015

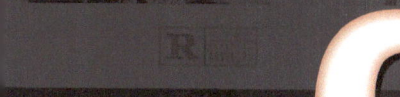

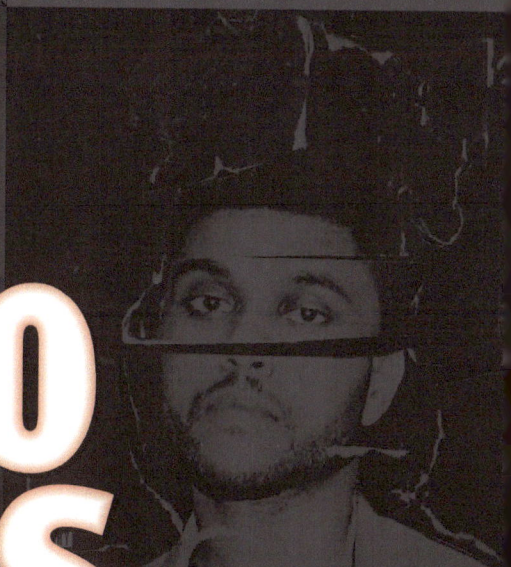

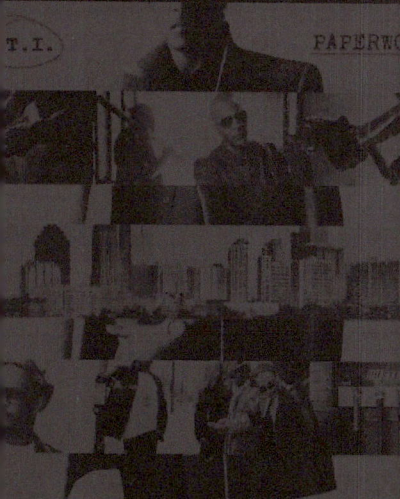

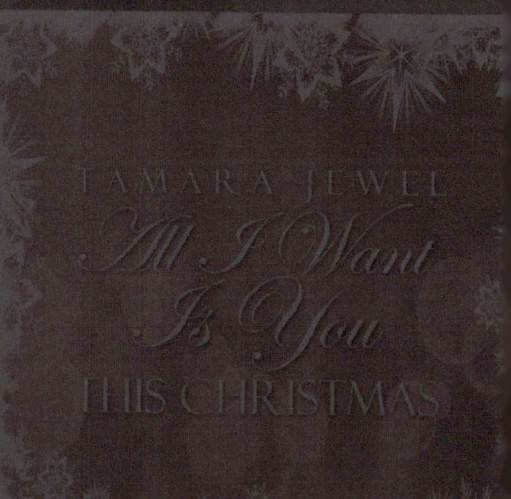

TOP 10 CHARTS

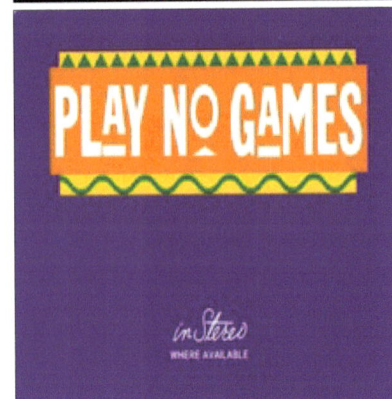

BIG SEAN - OPENING THE DETROIT LIONS FOOTBALL HALF-TIME SHOW WITH HIS HIT SINGLE.

SDM TOP 10 SINGLES CHART OF THE MONTH

No.	Artist - Song Title
1	BIG SEAN - PLAY NO GAMES
2	FETTY WAP - AGAIN
3	ESKO - MEAN SOMETHING
4	KENDRICK LAMAR - ALRIGHT
5	SCHOOLBOY Q - STUDIO
6	T.I. - PRIVATE SHOW FT. CHRIS BROWN
7	CHIEF 313 - WHY TRY
8	DRAKE - HOTLINE BLING
9	TAMARA JEWEL - ALL I WANT IS YOU THIS CHRISTMAS
10	RICH MOOK - YES I DO

SDM TOP 10 ALBUMS CHART OF THE MONTH

No.	Artist - Album Title
1	JEEZY - CHURCH IN THESE STREETS
2	TY DOLLA $IGN - FREE TC
3	THE WEEKND - BEAUTY BEHIND THE MADNESS
4	JANET - UNBREAKABLE
5	DRAKE & FUTURE - WHAT A TIME TO BE ALIVE
6	AYE MONEY - SUPPORT DETROIT MOVEMENT COMPILATION (VOLUME 1)
7	FETTY WAP - FETTY WAP
8	THE GAME - THE DOCUMENTARY 2
9	J. COLE - 2014 FOREST HILLS DRIVE
10	DRAKE - IF YOU'RE READING THIS IT'S TOO LATE

MMM

ARTIST: Diddy
REVIEWER: Cheraee C.
RATING: 4

The Bad Boy mogul P. Diddy has done it again with the release of the hottest album of the year "MMM." Diddy hasn't released a studio album in five years, but he still knows how to reinvent himself as an artist. The acronym MMM stands for Money Making Mitch. Mitch as in the fictional character depicted in 2002's Paid in Full, and a realistic drug dealer from Harlem, Rich Porter. The album includes over 10 features from the hottest mc's and producers in the game including French Montana, Rick Ross, Lil Kim, Big Sean, and more. Every track is a banger and complements every generation of music. Your bound to download and put that album on replay.

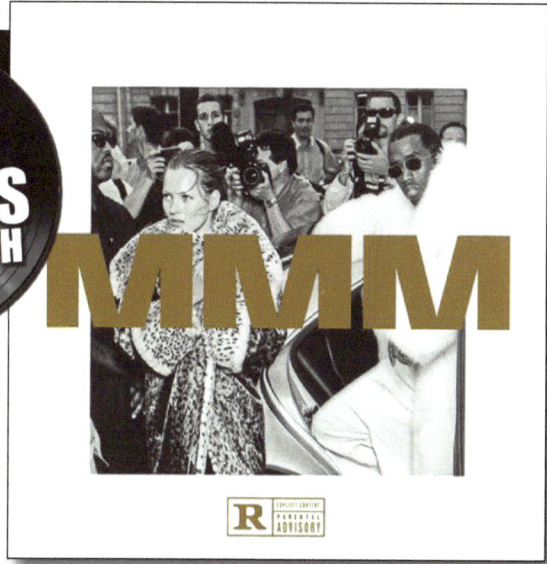

TOP 3 ALBUMS THIS MONTH

MMM

R EXPLICIT CONTENT PARENTAL ADVISORY

RATE METER: 1 - WACK 2 - NEEDS WORK 3 - STRAIGHT 4 - BANGER 5 - CLASSIC

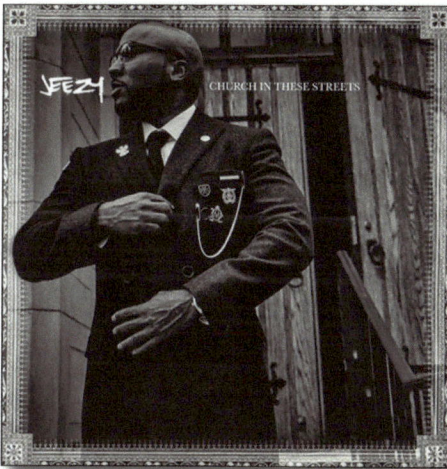

Church In These Streets

ARTIST: Jeezy
REVIEWER: Motowndiva
RATING: 4

Trap music with a spiritual vibe. Jeezy kills the scene again with his picture of reality. While painting pictures of drugs, violence, and money in his hood, Jeezy completes another classic. Church in These Streets is a banger and exactly what Jeezy is known for creating.

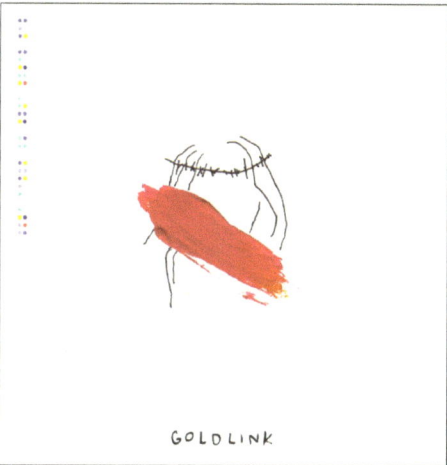

And After That We Didn't Talk

ARTIST: GoldLink
REVIEWER: Motowndiva
RATING: 4

This is not your typical Hip Hop album. It's a slick mix of songs you can dance to, conscious thoughts, and love stories. Overall the album has something for everyone and it's all delivered with GoldLink's wicked poetic flow. Don't sleep on this young artist from the DMV.

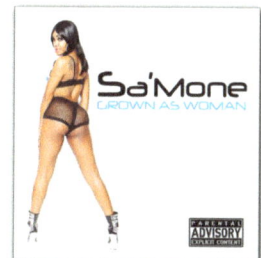

HEELS &
SKILLZ

Miss Fare

Orlando FL. Also Seen
in Smooth Magazine
(cover), KING magazine
2x, Bare Arms Cover
Model, Show Maga-
zine, Segrams Calendar
Model, Monster Energy
spokes model.

instagram
@missfarenw

Photography by
@treagenkier

HEELS & SKILLZ

Gina Smilez
also seen in Bare Arms
BAD calendar, Don Diva
and Fyne Girls Magazine.

Instagram
@ginasmilez

Photography by
@treagenkier

HEELS & SKILLZ

Photography by
@treagenkier

Detroit vs. Detroit

HOW BAD BUSINESS IS DETROYING DETROIT'S NETWORKING CIRCLE.

by Cheraee C.

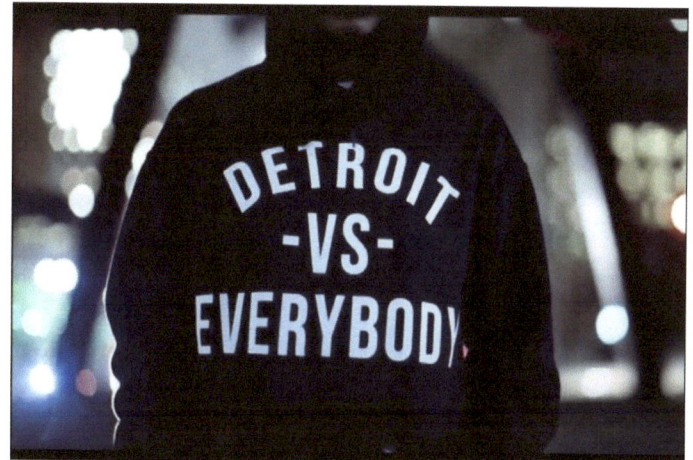

When you dissect a city full of giftedness, arrogance and competitiveness are two opposing variables destroying our population. Black's not supporting each other is at an ultimate high and most industries are becoming overcrowded with people who share the same craft. People are willing to subject themselves to shadiness for the price of fame. Everybody wants to be the CEO of a business but no one wants to work hard to earn that title. Instead of affirmative networking, people down talk and downplay each other. As a result, of the shade we become discriminatory towards our kind.

Why is it so much hate in our city? Detroit is the only city that hates on one another for wanting to be successful. Hoodrich celebs are all over the internet misrepresenting themselves with borrowed goods and fake money. If you broke you broke; if you rich you rich, so your image doesn't need to be classified because it speaks for itself.

Not only are we at war with our mentality, but we are at war with each other. The only wars we fight should be over freedom, laws, or rights not over J's, popular frames, etc. If you want a luxury, get a hustle, and work towards that luxury. Another person's lifestyle whether high or low should be out of sight and out of mind.

So while Everybody is walking around wearing Detroit vs. Everybody attire which is a huge facade, the real reality of Detroiter's is Detroit vs. Detroit. Where's the support? Everybody wants to get support, but nobody wants to give it. Let's support one another's movement and respect the hustles we believe in.

NEXT 2 BLOW

ESKO IS RIDING ON A NEW WAVE WITH HIS NEW HIT SINGLE "MEAN SOMETHING".

I t's a new wave in street rap and his swag is blazing from the eastside of Detroit. Mocy Music Group has a brand new artist best known as Detroit Esko. It's a lot of rappers in the game using the name Esko, but Detroit's Esko has a wavy style that's ideal and unfiltered.

In December 2015, Esko is getting ready to drop his first mixtape titled "White Line Feva." Some current singles from his upcoming EP include "New Wave," the street banger "Mean Something," "TFRU," and "Ten Shots." Esko's music is available on Soundcloud, iTunes, Amazon, and YouTube. You can also listen to music from Esko on the Support Detroit Movement Compilation Vol 1 and 2.

In the past, Esko was involved with a group called Future Empire and a label called Swat Legion. Due to different views on music and distance in between members, Esko has been solo dolo. Unlike most artists, Esko will never forget where he came from. In light of that Esko doesn't have any bad blood with either group and still represents Swat Legion even though he has made a new connection. With the support of Mocy Music Group, Esko's music career will advance to the next level.

You can stay connected with Esko on Facebook @Jesus Esko, Instagram @detroitesko, and on Twitter @itsyobabymybaby. Stay tuned because more music from this dope Detroit rapper is coming soon.

Esko - Mean Something
(Mocy Music Group)

Bringing a brand new ambience to the female lanes of the music industry is a sassy, female MC by the name of Jade Judo. She is a songwriter, lyricist, actress, model, and a rapper from Detroit's Brightmo area. She considers her musical genre to be R&B/trap music. Her sound is very original mixed with her Black and Filipino background, sexy, fierce, and emotional.

Jade's music is available on Soundcloud, ReverbNation, and YouTube, and her music will soon be available on iTunes. Her third mixtape "The Greenprint" is expected to drop January 2016. Her first mixtape was released in 2008 titled "Unleashed" and her second mixtape was released in 2012 called "Public Eye." Currently, in heavy rotation on YouTube you can check out her two latest videos which are "Cold Yea Yea" featuring the Detroit rapper and producer Icey, "Holographic Bedroom," and her single "Love and Pain." All of these records are track bangers you want to add to your playlist ASAP. In the Detroit area, Jade has worked with Detroit artists including Helluva, Young Gator, Bread Boi Foe, Monte, Mal Amani, and Neishanashae. Throughout her path to success, she has met a lot of celebrities including Ray J, Baby Blue from Pretty Ricky, Zues Irons, floss-a-lot from Tandbfilms, and many more.

Far from your traditional female rapper, Jade is an unsigned artist striving for eminence. Prospectively, she plans to keep dropping music, videos, release an album, and collaborate with some industry heavy hitters such as Wiz Khalifa. Although, the Jade runway is thriving, investing and networking takes time, but eventually Jade

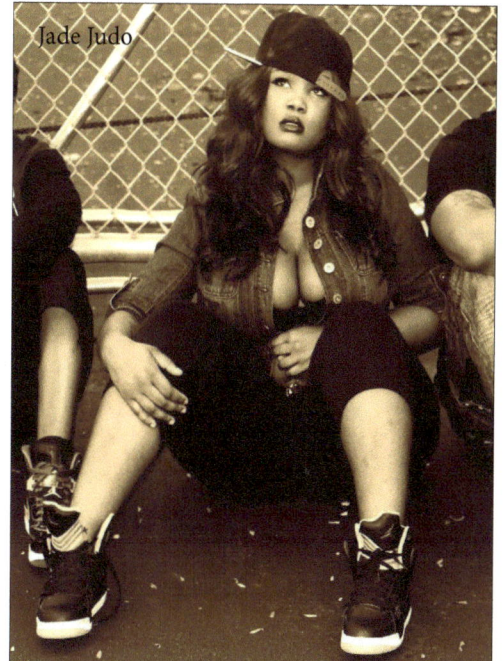
Jade Judo

will make the right industry connections to score more levels in her music career.

Please follow Jade on Instagram, Facebook, and Twitter as Jade Judo and watch her come-up.

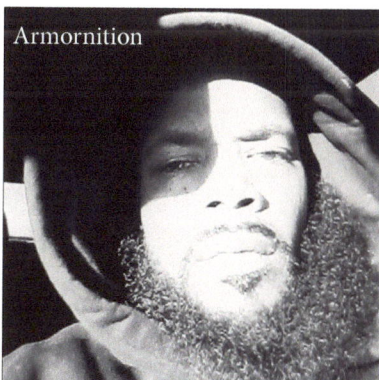
Armornition

Get your fire hydrated for a very opinionated, self-made artist from the westside of Detroit known as Armornition. He is a rapper, a producer, a ghost-writer, and the founder of his own label Bankroll Ent, which he started in 2013. His label promotes an array of talent from singing, dancing, rapping, comedy, etc. In 2016, Armor's label will be dropping two fresh artists whose names are Billion Dollar Gang and Meez Swith.

Armor's music gives insightful revelations and messages about day to day struggles coming from a man's perspective. Armornition travels the world showcasing his talent, and his top 3 cities include Detroit, Flint, and Vegas.

Actively. Armornition is multi-tasking on three different projects. The first project is his mixtape titled "The Cure" which he will be releasing December 2015 features Detroit artist The One. The second mixtape is titled "Finally I Arrive" which will be released January 2016 with features from Detroit artists King Dillon, Forty Da Great, and AR Da Kernel. The third mixtape featuring DGE is titled "I Got Questions & I Want Answers" which will also be released December 2015. Prior to these projects Armor released Now or Never EP in 2013 which includes the hit single "Better Know Thatt" featuring Black Chief and "Man Up." Next in line he released Victory EP in July 2015.

There are so many challenges in the music industry especially being an entrepreneur. One of Armor's biggest challenges is having money for funding because it takes money to make money. Another challenge is creating a strong support system: giving support is easy, but getting support is often a hassle. Every force needs a team with its key players working behind closed doors, but eventually Armornition will make the right connections and reach higher peaks in his musical succession.

Armornition's music is available in major music stores including Tidal, Google Play, iTunes, Soundcloud, YouTube, etc. If you are interested in buying beats from Armornition, you can purchase beats at www.banginbeatzpro.com. Stay hip to this artist on Twitter @Tnition, Instagram @armornition, and Facebook @Armor Nition. You can also stay connected to Armornition through his website www.armornition.com.

SNAP SHOTS

SNAP SHOTS

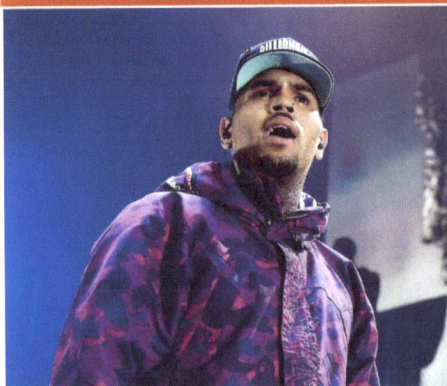

SNAP SHOTS

Email Your Snap Shots to
snapshots@sdmlive.com

The tablet computer

THE IPAD PRO IS ON THE MARKET AND PACKED WITH GOODY'S A 30 YEAR OLD WOULD JUMP FOR JOY OVER.

by Casino B.

The New iPad Pro is really big (almost 13 inches diagonally). It's what everyone says when they see it. The iPad has always offered a uniquely first-class quality experience. And now with the new 12.9-inch Retina display and nearly double the CPU speed performance of iPad Air 2, the iPad Pro adds another dimension to its great experience.

So if you're on the go, business or pleasure, you will love the iPad Pro to handle all your professional needs.

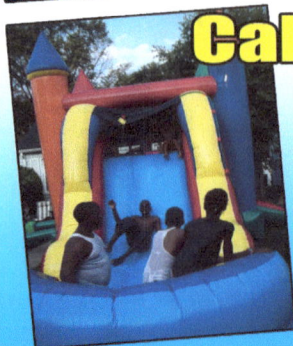

WE HAVE THE LOWEST PRINTING PRICES IN THE NATION

250 EVENT TICKETS
FULL-COLOR ON BOTH SIDES ON THICK UV COATED 14 PT

only $45

1000 BUSINESS CARDS
FULL-COLOR ON BOTH SIDES ON THICK UV COATED 14 PT

only $25

1000 4X6 CLUB FLYERS
FULL-COLOR ON BOTH SIDES ON THICK UV COATED 14 PT

only $65

Need a Design? Add $20 for Business Card or $40 for Flyer

2x5ft VINYL BANNER
FULL-COLOR IN or OUTDOOR BANNER w/GROMMETS

only $99

5000 BUSINESS CARDS
FULL-COLOR ON BOTH SIDES ON THICK UV COATED 14 PT

only $99

2500 4X6 CLUB FLYERS
FULL-COLOR ON BOTH SIDES ON THICK UV COATED 14 PT

only $85

CHECK OUT MORE SPECIALS & ORDER ONLINE ANYTIME: WWW.5DSPRODUCTIONS.COM

1.888.718.2999

5DS PRODUCTIONS®
THE PRINT MEDIA CENTER.

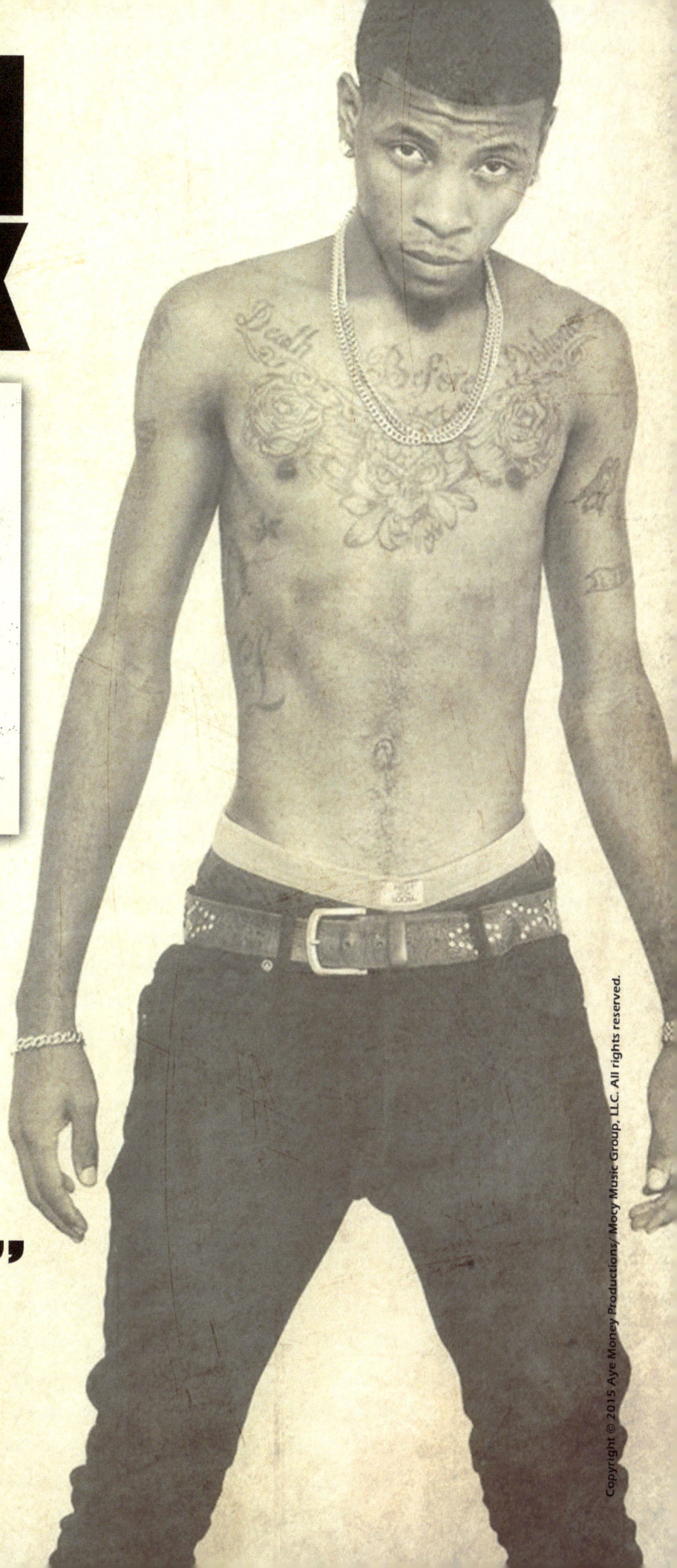

THE ALL NEW STYLE OF MAGAZINE-BOOKS

SDM

For advertisement
please call (586) 646-8505
or visit www.sdmlive.com

www.ingramcontent.com/pod-product-compliance
Lightning Source LLC
Chambersburg PA
CBHW040019050426
42452CB00002B/52